Messages

Caroline L Wilkes

Copyright © 2017 Caroline L Wilkes

All rights reserved.

ISBN:1975654676
ISBN-13:9781975654672

DEDICATION

This book is dedicated to my wonderful parents, Ron and Sylvia Wilkes, whose lives and deaths have taught me everything I need to know in order to be in this world without them.

It is also dedicated to every grieving heart in existence.

CONTENTS

Preface	i - iii
Poetry & verse	1 - 39
About the author	41

PREFACE

I would like to start by thanking you for trusting in 'Messages'. For whatever reason you're reading this little book, it means a lot to me to have you here. And I'd like to tell you why I decided to publish my words on grief and loss.

Put simply, it's because I have lost and I know how it feels to step daily into the nightmare instead of waking from it. I know the unrelenting wheel of pain you find yourselves upon the very moment someone you love dies, and the desperation and sense of madness that comes in doing so.

The light does come. We all know it comes. We've all seen others survive. But that's only because the survivors have learned to hold the hand of grief, which in truth we are never rid of. How could we be? We never stop loving the person who has died, and grief is love.

My upbringing was a complicated one. I had wonderful parents but I was bullied in school and grew up wrapped in emotional pain. It was my mum who held and helped me through it all. She was my universe; the only person on the planet who understood me. Mum could look beyond the outside of me to find the inside. She was everything.

When I was 23 and she was 61, she collapsed three months after being diagnosed with cancer. She died in my arms at home on the floor. The only other person there at the time was my dad and together we had to share the horrifying images. I think it brought comfort to us both knowing that there was at least one other person in the world who had witnessed that hell.

Yet at the time I was calm and I never thought I would or could be. I was instructed to give my mum mouth to mouth resuscitation but it was useless. When the paramedics arrived, I stood aside to let them work on her, all the while staring at her

i

chest in the vain hope it would rise for another breath. Nothing happened and I had to surrender to the truth. But I came to believe that my beautiful mother gave her last breath to me for a reason. And I was determined to carry it well.

After such a profoundly raw trauma I had nightmares for four years yet I always knew that I needed to be amidst bereavement, potentially to help heal my own. If I could take mum's death and use it for the greater good then it was *for* something. With my love of writing I trained as a Funeral Celebrant.

My mum left in 2006 and it took me six years to find the strength to go forward with this wish, to reach a new plateau of survival. I researched grief, learnt about its effects, its fall-out and its many dimensions. I felt it, I walked with it, I asked other's questions about their own experiences. I was beginning to feel strong enough to support others.

My mother wasn't my first loss. Her brother - who I was very close to - died the year before and more recently in 2015 I lost my lovely dad. Yet losing mum was instrumental in shaping my life and character. The bullying combined with her loss made me a very empathic woman, and one who was unafraid of pain.

In my five years as a celebrant and briefly as a funeral director, I have discovered that grief often gets silenced, albeit unintentionally. The bereaved either feel their emotions make others feel awkward or they're pressured into 'getting over it'. "It's been six months, a year, five years…so why am I still crying?"

Many also suffer guilt for their anger towards someone who has died even if the death was not their fault. I've thrown my mum's photo across the room more times than I can remember and yelled at her for leaving. That's perfectly normal. If it makes you feel better throw pictures and apologise to the great Ether later on. I did. I sometimes laughed about how my mum's photo

MESSAGES

was so perfectly wedged between furniture and I knew she'd have found it amusing. Give yourselves a break. Grief is literally hell on earth.

All that I have learnt has come to me from living with bereavement and walking broken families through the early stages of theirs. I am honoured to be allowed into people's homes, to observe their private grief – and I love them for it.

Along the way I have been called to write poems, musings, thoughts and understandings and I wanted to put some of them into a book. So, here it is. Some pieces have been written from the perspective of the bereaved but many are in the forms of a message from those who have died, to those mourning their loss. This is because of the nature of writing funerals.

There will always be a human need to give a missing person a voice - one that so desperately needs to be heard by broken hearts of relatives and friends. I hope that some of my words might touch something within you and might speak to a part of you that's in need of support or understanding. Even if there is just one message you can take on your own journey then this little book is worthwhile.

Today, I am happy and I am in the light. I know how to walk with this grief and how to use it as a tool to deepen my own heart and find beauty in the simplest things. Loss has taught me so much about how to live, laugh, love and hope. Sometimes I cry…but that's ok.

Carry this book of messages with you, and realise that in the greater scheme of things you're not alone in your pain. Grief is lonely and dark but at some point the sun will rise again, the flowers will blossom and all will be bearable once more.

We spoke only few words
But the words that we spoke were

"I love you"

And they will do.

The void created within me when you moved into your
death is vast and wide.

But in it I have gathered the moon and the stars,
And amongst them breathes every breath of love you have
given to me.

I have held the universe within me since you died...
and there is still room for more.

I WAS THERE

I lived a content life with you.
And the quietness about me gave no want of song and
dance and sprite.
I was much more like the stillness of the night,
And the breeze which asks for nothing of the day.

But I was there.
And I was the backdrop of our years.
So familiar and so solid, yet now I cause your tears.
I know that nothing will ever be the same,
Except for the love I felt for you.

Choking in your hurt, the passing of my life,
Gives no want of song or words of light.
But venture to the stillness of the night,
To the breeze which shows presence in the day.

And remember that I was there…
That time will ease this heavy burdening pain.
That one day the sun will rise again,
And all will be bearable once more.

Do not allow the world's demands to pull and push you.
Do not allow other people's expectations to hurry you.
Do not allow another's inability to stand with pain make
you silence your own.

Your grief is a new path placed beneath your feet which
you have no choice but to walk.

And it is to be walked at your pace alone.

MESSAGES

I look to the stars to find you and ask where
you are all the time.
Where are you now?
Where are you?

My darling,
If only you knew how deeply I am within you now,
you'd know that when you're looking to the stars to find me,
we're gazing at the same stars together.

CAROLINE L WILKES

If you miss my presence and wish me to be close,
Go you to the rolling hills that tumble shades of green.
Or stand upon the steepest cliff that
guards an ocean scene.
Walk amidst the seasons of nature's changing hue,
And know that there you will feel me close to you.

MESSAGES

BECAUSE

Because I'm angry, you see.
Angry because you left me.
Be it your choice or not, you left.
And now I am bereft.

Because I'm angry, at you.
Angry because you're gone.
Of your control or not, you went.
And my sanity is spent.

And I'm angry, at others.
Angry because they say
that blame will never change your death,
my shouts are wasted breath.

But I'm angry, at me.
Angry because I know!
But I need a way to fight apart
the torment in my heart.

I'm angry, at you.
And broken because I love you.
Be it your choice or not, you've died.
And I've nowhere from this pain to hide,

This burning pain that stabs inside,
as I've cried
and I've cried
and I've cried.

CAROLINE L WILKES

I held it inside, my love and pride for you,
but with it I found no voice.

It wasn't intentional nor a conscious choice...
but rather a way of being.

My assumption was that you knew.
But for the times you may not,
Hear now that I loved you so deeply
that I could not find the words,
And instead was the best I could be.

SOMETIMES

Sometimes I'm lonely and talk to the moon.
I ask if he'll hold the empty room in my heart,
Because you should be breathing,
But instead I'm grieving for you.

Sometimes I linger outside in the night,
Allowing its shadows to shelter the light of my tears,
Because you should be breathing,
But instead I'm grieving for you.

And I wonder if the flowers
sleeping in their earthy beds
stretch their petals as your soul drifts by.
And I wonder when the sunrise
paints the sky a dusty red
if I'll know why.

Sometimes I'm fine as I hear the bird
whose song is so lovely and is seldom heard
in these hours.
We share the same choice:
To share our true voice in secret.

Yet, sometimes I feel that you hold my hand
And in that aloneness you come to stand by my heart.
You say I know you're grieving,
And I'm sorry for leaving,
But I am still breathing, sweetheart.

CAROLINE L WILKES

You are a rainbow,
created by the presence of sunshine
and raindrops.

So accept the good and
the bad moments,

for they are the making of your beauty.

MESSAGES

There is such sacredness within the elders of our world.
They're a generation so often overlooked, yet their minds
hold treasures disguised beneath weathered skin and
silvered hair.

If only we understood the brilliance hiding there.

Expected and elderly death does not diminish the value of
their life nor the magnitude of their loss. Whilst they are
here allow their wisdom to guide your youthful hearts.
And when they are gone carry their light within you
always.

Nothing is so deep as the souls of the
elders of our world.

IF I HAD A VOICE

If I had a voice now,
It would be loving,
And I would say thank you for all of your care.

If I had a voice now,
I'd want to tell you
I'm sorry for not always wanting to be there.

My life, it confused you. It did so to me.
But I am released now and my heart is free.
The heart that was hidden beneath all the pain,
It felt so much more than I could explain.

And if I had a voice now,
I'd say out loud,
I love you, I wish that I'd made that clear.

And in my lifetime
I need you to know
That I was much more than I did appear.

These are the things that I'd say through choice,
if I had the chance,
if I had a voice.

MESSAGES

I am from whence clouds of heather tuft grows,
Upon mountains purple and strong.
And I am from where bonnie tartan was born,
Where air carries swept bagpipe song.

I am from whence clans' ancestral voice
Echoes throughout trees and sand.
And now as my breath has taken its flight
And dances on breath of that land,

I must away for I cannot stay,
And I must let go of your hand.

CAROLINE L WILKES

In the darkest and greyest of days,
when my own thoughts echo because I feel so alone
without your life...
if there is ever any light to be seen,
no matter how humble or shy,
I know and I hope it to be you.

MESSAGES

TAPESTRY

My life, it was a tapestry of silken threads and hue.
And many times the weaving was filled
with love and care.

At times threads were woven not by me, but you.
And my colours would be lacking
had you not been there.

You represent the stitches, each day with me you spent,
And gradually a pattern around the edges grew.
Each year, another flower to friendship represent,
Each smile a leaf adorning my creation born of you.

My life, it was a tapestry of joy given to me,
Know your every kindness
it surely does behold.

And though the many colours are bright for all to see,
The love that you've bestowed
is stitched in threads of gold.

What is this closure that people speak of because I have
certainly never found it. I still love and adore those I have
lost and I don't ever want to feel an end to their absence,
as painful as it is.

Acceptance of their leaving...that's another matter.

We reach that when we are ready, when it is found
organically through a natural space of time that is
unavoidably travelled through.

After all, we can't stop the world from turning even
when we're grieving; even when we feel that ours' has
ended.

But closure?
No.
I will never shut a door on my grief. But I will open my
heart wider and love even more. I will talk to them always
though their answers are silent.

I will hold their memories to me so softly. As if I held the
most precious thing in the world within my arms. As if I
held the trust of a dove. And I will want to feel their life
and their death, forever.

MESSAGES

When I close my eyes and think of you,
we are always together.

My toes touch the seas as my fingers touch the planets,
and all in between is where we are.

It wasn't this easy when you first left. But now I realise
that our love fills the entire universe and I only have to
think of you to be there.

FALL AND RISE

Life at times may be like a stream,
Where days flow easy and under the beams
Of moonlight and stars, the night is a friend.
And hurts of the heart are easy to mend.

Life can also feel like a hill.
It takes all your strength and all of your will
To reach the horizon where sunlight shines down,
Over the sleepiness of country and town.

But when your path is filled with such treasure,
It gives you so much that you cannot measure.
The ups and the downs become not as dear
As the family whose hearts have always been near.

So though a life may fall and rise
Like swallows that swoop and soar through the skies,
Its love that is carried into forever,
And sadness releases as light as a feather.

When you've been loved by family care,
When you've been held in all they can share,
Regardless of ease or struggle of days,
You know you've been blessed in so many ways
And beauty is found in your yesterdays.

BEAUTY OF THE WAVES

Should you need to feel my presence
very close to you,
Venture to the wildish coasts
where sand and land meet blue.

For I have lived a life of tides
upon the waves at sea.
It's in the lines of foaming white
that holds the breath of me.

The swell, it tells of times
when I was brave and I was strong.
It lifts to voice the truth,
that sapphire days we shared were long.

The tide recedes to tell of times
when I was not so bold.
The sunlight painting whispers
of our love in amber gold.

So when you miss my warmth and care,
just wander to the ocean,
And find me there amidst the swirling
lapping of its motion.

And know that all I ever was
will not be found in graves,
For all I was will live within
the beauty of the waves.

It's in the quiet bluey-grey moments when I need you.
When my tears are silent and nobody sees.
And nobody knows that your face is everywhere
to me.

It's in these lonelinesses that I spend time
with you again.

When I dare to feel what lies inside,
this bluey-grey sadness
and this pain since you died.

COME WITH ME

Come with me, the one I love.
Let us find that memory,
The one that leads to truthful time
And falls upon simplicity.

Can you find that silken day
Amongst the winter's cold?
Can you see now what I meant...
Our love shall not grow old.

Close your eyes and see the glow
That blessed the evening sky.
Feel the peace we chose to feel,
That held us, you and I.

Can you see the country lane,
The ground of snowy lace?
And can you hear the words I spoke
As soft I held your face?

Now hold that memory to you,
We made it for this day.
I shall hold your hand again
And never fade away.

Now hold that memory to you,
For in it you shall find
A couple walking, holding hands,
Together in your mind.

I am not gone, I am not sad.
I have taken the good and forgotten the bad.
And now that I'm held in peace and in light,
I promise to shower my love in moonlight.
Forever you'll find my smile in the sun,
Shining down warmth upon everyone.
I love you, I see you, I comfort your fears.
I'm laughing and loving and drying your tears.

MESSAGES

INTERMENT BLESSING

Fleeting and precious this life passes,
And now we rest you amidst the grasses,
Where seasons shall hold all of your light,
Through sun of day and darkness of night.

And here you'll remain as years go by,
A place we can kneel and smile and cry,
A place to remember the love you would share,
A place to treasure and touch with our care.

And now as we give your body to earth,
Forever grateful for your sacred birth.
Forever we'll hold the memories too,
And whisper our prayers in honour of you.

If you do speak to the grieving amongst us,
let your words be honest and gentle; not seeking to ease
pain but to validate it.

There are no words that can soften grief, but in the
allowing of its presence within your sincere company, it
can be held...gifting the bereaved with a momentary breath
beneath its accumulating weight.

MESSAGES

MY MEMORY IN YOUR HAND

Don't speak of gentle rainbows
and white clouds when I die.
Don't go sharing how I'm somewhere
flying in the sky.

You know I wouldn't 'sentiment'
over my own death.
I am much more present
in the breathing of your breath…

In the songs I used to listen to,
in the wine I loved to drink,
in the way I conquered hardship,
pushing limits to the brink.

I don't live outside of you
for I refuse to leave.
I am the strength inside your heart
that lifts you as you grieve.

Don't speak of angels singing,
of places far away.
Don't go talking of a land
that you will join one day.

I'm already with you
for I am in your mind.
When you feel I'm missing
and you're almost walking blind,
Have the faith to take that step
and feel my love demand
That for my sake you must walk on
with my memory in your hand.

25

HEART-SHAPED

Looking down upon your tired body,
Watching you laying in your bed.
Me standing at your precious feet
And angels gathered at your head.

Time is moving too fast and too slowly,
You look like you but now so holy
And I'm wondering if I can let go.
Will I be able to let you go?

Sitting here in silence I get to thinking
Of how I'll breathe when you're gone.
It's not right that I ask you to stay,
It's not fair to keep you holding on.

Time is moving too fast and too slowly,
You look like you but now so holy.
You look like saints and sacred paintings,
I'll sing to you just while you're waiting.

I wish you a heart-shaped journey as you pass,
I wish for you to be reflected
in the colours of stained glass.
I wish for you to be carried to the noblest star,
I'll wish you heart-shaped everything from afar.

I feel your breathing start to linger
My heart beats fast as yours slows down.
I see the beings of past in pastels,
Hear harmonies of Ethereal sound.

Cont'd…

MESSAGES

And now the time is neither too fast or slow,
Its simply just the time when you're meant to go,
And grace befalls upon this moment of peace
as I watch your soul find the release.

I see you're heart-shaped as your light expands above,
Your soul is as heart-shaped
as the purest breath of love.
And because of all you gave to me when you were here,
I wish you heart-shaped everything through my tears.

"Dry those eyes" I hear you say to me,
"I heard every wish you made before my soul was free.
And now my journey is heart-shaped in every way,
But my greatest gift lay hidden in you every day."

I dried my eyes enough to watch you leave,
My heart caught fire as it learnt what it was to grieve.
But before you left I saw within this darkest night,
A reflection of myself within your golden light,
The gift of your everyday through the eyes of you,

I saw that I am heart-shaped too.
I saw that I am heart-shaped too.

CAROLINE L WILKES

Spend not too many breaths asking where I am,
For you know that the answer is everywhere.
As long as there are robins and flowers in gardens,
And for as long as the sun warms your face,
I will be found in all that matters,
not in one single place,
But in all that is beautiful to you.

MESSAGES

What people must understand is that once you have lost someone who has been a significant part of your life and more importantly, your heart, you cannot be fully who you were before.

As life has shaped you, so will grief. So try not to yield beneath the expectations of others into being who they once knew.

You simply are not...and you don't have to be.

You're in pain, you're beautiful as you are and you're becoming. You don't know what you're becoming, but it's something deeper than before.

CAROLINE L WILKES

The simple things that I once loved
I now give for you to tend,
And trust that you will softly care
For garden's faithful feathered friend.

And as you gift the birds with love
And keep them fed in winter's snow,
You will be holding me at heart,
More than you could ever know.

Remember me within their joy,
Listen for me in sweet refrain,
And there you'll hear familiar voice…
There you'll feel me close again.

MESSAGES

At the root of everything that matters is love.
We often view grief as a negative thing, something we
need to get over, finish, run away from.

Yes, it is painful...but it is born of love. And if we're
honest, if the only way to end the pain was to end the love
we'd shared, we'd choose to keep the love and the pain,
and bear it like the brave and extraordinary bereaved
beings that we are.

Like we do. Every single day.

It is often so true that we deepen in grief. We take on an empathy that can only ever be born of pain and when we are ready to lift our heads above the water again to say hello to the world, we emerge changed and with even more beautiful hearts than before.

The beauty in every heartache...is us.

NO MORE OF ME MISSING

I know it feels to you my dear,
That so much time has passed
Since you had all of me here,
Since I knew you last.

I never would have ever left
The way my illness insisted.
And goodness knows the ways in which
My strength of mind resisted.

But now it's time for you to gather
Your memories of me.
The ones I lost some time ago
When forced to set them free.

And know that deep within my heart,
You always were the light,
That saved my emptiness from cold
Through dementia's night.

Gather me whole inside you now,
It's time for reminiscing.
At last complete inside your minds,
There's no more of me missing.

You may even see the one who has died in a completely different light and the reasons behind their actions may have been gifted with a little more clarity than ever before. That is a beautiful thing. Because when we die, to be recognised and understood in all our truth is the final blossoming of the relationship we shared with those we leave behind.

MESSAGES

A FATHER'S STANCE

Sturdy as my masculine stance,
the rocks and paths have carried me miles,
reflecting the strength within my bones,
through many brooks, o'er many stiles.

But strength of flesh and body be
not where my greatest power lay,
'twas my heart in humble tones
that saw me through each night and day.

Resilient as the moors at dusk,
as boulders trampled by the weather.
Protecting all about my feet
the innocent blooms of child-like heather.

My stance held like an ancient pillar,
refused to crumble, refused to fall.
For I had children gazing up
for whom I must always stand tall.

Now they've grown and stretched up high,
to bear the weather of their years,
I have melted back to earth
to hold the raindrops of their tears.

The way I loved, the way I walked,
the life I lived with all my might,
still rumbles on like tumbling tremors
of endless thunder in the night.
And you will feel me in your hearts,
steering you from wrong to right.

35

It's in the sunshine where you'll find me now,
Lighting your worlds from a different place
Of channelled strength and endless space.

My warmth will lift you from the ground
and point to horizons waiting for you.
I'll push you still in all that you do.

It's in the sunshine where you'll feel my presence,
Loving you with the entirety of sky,
Holding you in the breadth of my power,
guiding you through every minute and hour.
And beneath my rays you'll flourish and flower.
I'll leave you no choice.

Carry my heart.
Remember my voice.

MESSAGES

When the earthshine smiles down upon me
from the watchful moon
and gifts to me a star from your sky,
I immerse myself within your love
and know that you are the light in the dark,
always.

GO NOW

Go now into those hills.
Where the sun meets the land with its permanent spills
Of orangey glows and promise of dawn.
Be part of the sunrise as each day is born.

Go now, go to the lakes.
Where the water of glassy light mirrors the sky.
Where freedom and memory breathe through the land
And those gone before take hold of your hand.

Go now to where you can wander,
Where your warrior spirit can now take some rest.
Camp under the stars, your battles are through.
There's only adventure waiting for you.

But just look behind to where you once lived,
To the pride we feel in all that you were…
Respecting you more than perhaps you did know.
But now it's your time and we must let you go.

MESSAGES

THE FAIRIES AND THE TREES

Through the clouds your spirit came
to live and be given a different name.
But you walk within flowers in your sleep,
Dance with the fairies in woods of deep
and shady trees.
And dip your toes in crystal streams,
Then flutter your soul through trees and sunbeams.

You hold the birds within your hands
And sing a song from where you stand...
Upon a height, gazing out to sea,
Your soul a bird with wings to be free.
A world where nature is your home,
An ancient green land you're free to roam.

A world only your spirit knows,
Where bluebells and snowdrops and violets grow.
A life that only you can see
when your eyes are closed and your mind is free.
A place that lives beyond your sighs,
In distant, clear summer blue skies.

Your spirit soars throughout the hills
of pretty clover and daffodils.
A place that is always there,
A place behind a door
that opens when in your eyes
hazy sleep does pour.
Your spirit's home forever,
Within the nature your heart believes,
Amongst the fairies and the trees.

Written for my beautiful mother, Sylvia

40

ABOUT THE AUTHOR

Caroline Wilkes was born in 1982 and raised in Shrewsbury, Shropshire. Leaving her hometown in 2013 to build upon her vocation and career in bereavement, she worked as a Funeral Director whilst living in London and Wiltshire. She has since returned to the West Midlands and serves the communities of Birmingham and the surrounding counties.

Caroline loves to be out in nature and finds peace and solace amongst woodlands, where she can restore the energy given out in her work. She also has the wonderful companionship of her rescued Greyhound, Arwen.

Printed in Great Britain
by Amazon